BEOWULF AND GRENDEL

A VERSE TRANSLATION BY
MICHAEL ALEXANDER

D0587090

PENGUIN BOOKS

PENGUIN BOOKS

Published by the Penguin Group
Penguin Books Ltd, 27 Wrights Lane, London W8 5TZ, England
Penguin Books USA Inc., 375 Hudson Street, New York, New York 10014, USA
Penguin Books Australia Ltd, Ringwood, Victoria, Australia
Penguin Books Canada Ltd, 10 Alcorn Avenue, Toronto, Ontario, Canada M4V 3B2
Penguin Books (NZ) Ltd, 182–190 Wairau Road, Auckland 10, New Zealand

Penguin Books Ltd, Registered Offices: Harmondsworth, Middlesex, England

These selections are from Michael Alexander's translation of
Beowulf, published in Penguin Classics 1973
This edition published 1995
1 3 5 7 9 10 8 6 4 2

Printed in England by Clays Ltd, St Ives plc

Attend!
We have heard of the thriving of the throne of
   Denmark,
how the folk-kings flourished in former days,
how those royal athelings earned that glory.

Was it not *Scyld Shefing* that shook the halls,
took mead-benches, taught encroaching
foes to fear him—who, found in childhood,
lacked clothing? Yet he lived and prospered,
grew in strength and stature under the heavens
until the clans settled in the sea-coasts neighbouring
over the whale-road all must obey him
and give tribute. He was a good king!

A boy child was afterwards born to Scyld,
a young child in hall-yard, a hope for the people,
sent them by God; the griefs long endured
were not unknown to Him, the harshness of years
without a lord. Therefore the Life-bestowing

Wielder of Glory granted them this blessing.
Through the northern lands the name of Beow,
the son of Scyld, sprang widely.
For in youth an atheling should so use his virtue,
give with a free hand while in his father's house,
that in old age, when enemies gather,
established friends shall stand by him
and serve him gladly. It is by glorious action
that a man comes by honour in any people.

At the hour shaped for him Scyld departed,
the hero crossed into the keeping of his Lord.
They carried him out to the edge of the sea,
his sworn arms-fellows, as he had himself desired them
while he wielded his words, Warden of the Scyldings,
beloved folk-founder; long had he ruled.

A boat with a ringed neck rode in the haven,
icy, out-eager, the atheling's vessel,
and there they laid out their lord and master,
dealer of wound gold, in the waist of the ship,
in majesty by the mast. A mound of treasures
from far countries was fetched aboard her,
and it is said that no boat was ever more bravely fitted
   out
with the weapons of a warrior, war accoutrement,

swords and body-armour; on his breast were set
treasures and trappings to travel with him
on his far faring into the flood's sway.

This hoard was not less great than the gifts he had had
from those who at the outset had adventured him
over seas, alone, a small child.

High over head they hoisted and fixed
a gold *signum*; gave him to the flood,
let the seas take him, with sour hearts
and mourning mood. Men under heaven's
shifting skies, though skilled in counsel,
cannot say surely who unshipped that cargo.

Then for a long space there lodged in the stronghold
Beowulf the Dane, dear king of his people,
famed among nations—his father had taken
leave of the land—when late was born to him
the lord Healfdene, lifelong the ruler
and war-feared patriarch of the proud Scyldings.
He next fathered four children
that leaped into the world, this leader of armies,
Heorogar and *Hrothgar* and Halga the Good;
and Ursula, I have heard, who was Onela's queen,
knew the bed's embrace of the Battle-Scylfing.

Then to Hrothgar was granted glory in battle,
mastery of the field; so friends and kinsmen
gladly obeyed him, and his band increased
to a great company. It came into his mind
that he would command the construction
of a huge mead-hall, a house greater
than men on earth ever had heard of,
and share the gifts God had bestowed on him
upon its floor with folk young and old—
apart from public land and the persons of slaves.
Far and wide (as I heard) the work was given out
in many a tribe over middle earth,
the making of the mead-hall. And, as men reckon,
the day of readiness dawned very soon
for this greatest of houses. *Heorot* he named it
whose word ruled a wide empire.
He made good his boast, gave out rings,
arm-bands at the banquet. Boldly the hall reared
its arched gables; unkindled the torch-flame
that turned it to ashes. The time was not yet
when the blood-feud should bring out again
sword-hatred in sworn kindred.

It was with pain that the powerful spirit
dwelling in darkness endured that time,
hearing daily the hall filled

with loud amusement; there was the music of the harp,
the clear song of the poet, perfect in his telling
of the remote first making of man's race.
He told how, long ago, the Lord formed Earth,
a plain bright to look on, locked in ocean,
exulting established the sun and the moon
as lights to illumine the land-dwellers
and furnished forth the face of Earth
with limbs and leaves. Life He then granted
to each kind of creature that creeps and moves.

So the company of men led a careless life,
all was well with them: until One began
to encompass evil, an enemy from hell.
Grendel they called this cruel spirit,
the fell and fen his fastness was,
the march his haunt. This unhappy being
had long lived in the land of monsters
since the Creator cast them out
as kindred of *Cain*. For that killing of Abel
the eternal Lord took vengeance.
There was no joy of that feud: far from mankind
God drove him out for his deed of shame!
From Cain came down all kinds misbegotten
—ogres and elves and evil shades—

as also the Giants, who joined in long
wars with God. He gave them their reward.

With the coming of night came Grendel also,
sought the great house and how the Ring-Danes
held their hall when the horn had gone round.
He found in Heorot the force of nobles
slept after supper, sorrow forgotten,
the condition of men. Maddening with rage,
he struck quickly, creature of evil:
grim and greedy, he grasped on their pallets
thirty warriors, and away he was out of there,
thrilled with his catch: he carried off homeward
his glut of slaughter, sought his own halls.
As the day broke, with the dawn's light
Grendel's outrage was openly to be seen:
night's table-laughter turned to morning's
lamentation. Lord Hrothgar
sat silent then, the strong man mourned,
glorious king, he grieved for his thanes
as they read the traces of a terrible foe,
a cursed fiend. That was too cruel a feud,
too long, too hard!

      Nor did he let them rest
but the next night brought new horrors,

did more murder, manslaughter and outrage
and shrank not from it: he was too set on these things.

It was not remarked then if a man looked
for sleeping-quarters quieter, less central,
among the outer buildings; now openly shown,
the new hall-thane's hatred was manifest
and unmistakable. Each survivor
then kept himself at safer distance.

So Grendel became ruler; against right he fought,
one against all. Empty then stood
the best of houses, and for no brief space;
for twelve long winters torment sat
on the Friend of the Scyldings, fierce sorrows
and woes of every kind; which was not hidden
from the sons of men, but was made known
in grieving songs, how Grendel warred
long on Hrothgar, the harms he did him
through wretched years of wrong, outrage
and persecution. Peace was not in his mind
towards any companion of the court of Hrothgar,
the feud was not abated, the blood-price was unpaid.
Nor did any counsellor have cause to look for
a bright man-price at the murderer's hand:
the dark death-shadow drove always against them,

old and young; abominable
he watched and waited for them, walked nightlong
the misty moorland. Men know not
where hell's familiars fleet on their errands!

Again and again the enemy of man
stalking unseen, struck terrible
and bitter blows. In the black nights
he camped in the hall, under Heorot's gold roof;
yet he could not touch the treasure-throne
against the Lord's will, whose love was unknown to
  him.
A great grief was it for the Guardian of the Scyldings,
crushing to his spirit. The council lords
sat there daily to devise some plan,
what might be best for brave-hearted
Danes to contrive against these terror-raids.
They prayed aloud, promising sometimes
on the altars of their idols unholy sacrifices
if the Slayer of souls would send relief
to the suffering people.

                         Such was their practice,
a heathen hope; Hell possessed
their hearts and minds: the Maker was unknown to
  them,
the Judge of all actions, the Almighty was unheard of,

they knew not how to praise the Prince of Heaven,
the Wielder of Glory.

                Woe to him who must
in terrible trial entrust his soul
to the embrace of the burning, banished from thought
of change or comfort! Cheerful the man
able to look to the Lord at his death-day,
to find peace in the Father's embrace!
This season rocked the son of Healfdene
with swingeing sorrows; nor could the splendid man
put his cares from him. Too cruel the feud,
too strong and long-lasting, that struck that people,
a wicked affliction, the worst of nightmares!

This was heard of at his home by one of *Hygelac*'s
    followers,
a good man among the Geats, Grendel's raidings;
he was for main strength of all men foremost
that trod the earth at that time of day;
build and blood matched.

                He bade a seaworthy
wave-cutter be fitted out for him; the warrior king
he would seek, he said, over swan's riding,
that lord of great name, needing men.

The wiser sought to dissuade him from voyaging
hardly or not at all, though they held him dear;
they whetted his quest-thirst, watched omens.
The prince had already picked his men
from the folk's flower, the fiercest among them
that might be found. With fourteen men
he sought sound-wood; sea-wise *Beowulf*
led them right down to the land's edge.

Time running on, she rode the waves now,
hard in by headland. Harnessed warriors
stepped on her stem; setting tide churned
sea with sand, soldiers carried
bright mail-coats to the mast's foot,
war-gear well-wrought; willingly they shoved her
    out,
thorough-braced craft, on the craved voyage.

Away she went over a wavy ocean,
boat like a bird, breaking seas,
wind-whetted, white-throated,
till the curved prow had ploughed so far
—the sun standing right on the second day—
that they might see land loom on the skyline,
then the shimmer of cliffs, sheer fells behind,
reaching capes.

The crossing was at an end;
closed the wake. Weather-Geats
stood on strand, stepped briskly up;
a rope going ashore, ring-mail clashed,
battle-girdings. God they thanked
for the smooth going over the salt-trails.

The watchman saw them. From the wall where he
   stood,
posted by the Scyldings to patrol the cliffs,
he saw the polished lindens pass along the gangway
and the clean equipment. Curiosity
moved him to know who these men might be.

Hrothgar's thane, when his horse had picked
its way down to the shore, shook his spear
fiercely at arm's length, framed the challenge:
'Strangers, you have steered this steep craft
through the sea-ways, sought our coast.
I see you are warriors; you wear that dress now.
I must ask who you are.

                    In all the years
I have lived as look-out at land's end here
—so that no foreigners with a fleet-army
might land in Denmark and do us harm—

shield-carriers have never come ashore
more openly. You had no assurance
of welcome here, word of leave
from Hrothgar and *Hrothulf*!

                    I have not in my life
set eyes on a man with more might in his frame
than this helmed lord. He's no hall-fellow
dressed in fine armour, or his face belies him;
he has the head of a hero.
                    I'll have your names now
and the names of your fathers; or further you shall not
   go
as undeclared spies in the Danish land.
Stay where you are, strangers, hear
what I have to say! Seas crossed,
it is best and simplest straightaway to acknowledge
where you are from, why you have come.'

The captain gave him a clear answer,
leader of the troop, unlocked his word-hoard:
'We here are come from the country of the Geats
and are King Hygelac's hearth-companions.
My noble father was known as Edgetheow,
a front-fighter famous among nations,
who had seen many seasons when he set out at last

an old man from the halls; all the wiser men
in the world readily remember him.

It is with loyal and true intention that we come
to seek your lord of the son of Healfdene,
guardian of the people: guide us well therefore!
We have a great errand to the glorious hero,
the Shepherd of the Danes; the drift of it
shall not be kept from you. You must know if
   indeed
there is truth in what is told in Geatland,
that among the Scyldings some enemy,
an obscure assailant in the opaque night-times,
makes spectacles of spoil and slaughter
in hideous feud. To Hrothgar I would
openheartedly unfold a plan
how the old commander may overcome his foe;
if indeed an easing is ever to slacken
these besetting sorrows, a settlement
when chafing cares shall cool at last.
Otherwise he must miserably live out
this lamentable time, for as long as Heorot,
best of houses, bulks to the sky.'

The mounted coastguard made reply,
unshrinking officer: 'A sharp-witted man,

clear in his mind, must be skilled
to discriminate deeds and words.
I accept what I am told, that this troop is loyal
to the Scyldings' Protector. Pass forward with your
weapons and war-dress! I am willing to guide you,
commanding meanwhile the men under me
to guard with care this craft of yours,
this new-tarred boat at its berth by our strand
against every enemy until again it bear
its beloved captain over the current sea,
curve-necked keel, to the coasts of the Geat;
such a warrior shall be accorded
unscathed passage through the shocks of battle.'

The vessel was still as they set forward,
the deep-chested ship, stayed at its mooring,
fast at its anchor. Over the cheek-pieces
boar-shapes shone out, bristling with gold,
blazing and fire-hard, fierce guards
of their bearers' lives. Briskly the men went
marching together, making out at last
the ample eaves adorned with gold:
to earth's men the most glorious
of houses under heaven, the home of the king;
its radiance lighted the lands of the world.
The coastguard showed them the shining palace,

the resort of heroes, and how they might
rightly come to it; this captain in the wars
then brought his horse about, and broke silence:
'Here I must leave you. May the Lord Almighty
afford His grace in your undertakings
and bring you to safety. Back at the sea-shore
I resume the watch against sea-raiders.'

There was stone paving on the path that brought
the war-band on its way. The war-coats shone
and the links of hard hand-locked iron
sang in their harness as they stepped along
in their gear of grim aspect, going to the hall.
Sea-wearied, they then set against the wall
their broad shields of special temper,
and bowed to bench, battle-shirts clinking,
the war-dress of warriors. The weapons of the seamen
stood in the spear-rack, stacked together,
an ash-wood grey-tipped. These iron-shirted men
were handsomely armed.

        A high-mannered chieftain
then inquired after the ancestry of the warriors.
'From whence do you bring these embellished shields,
grey mail-shirts, masked helmets,
this stack of spears? I am spokesman here,

herald to Hrothgar; I have not seen
a body of strangers bear themselves more proudly.
It is not exile but adventure, I am thinking,
boldness of spirit, that brings you to Hrothgar.'

The gallant Geat gave answer then,
valour-renowned, and vaunting spoke,
hard under helmet: 'At Hygelac's table
we are sharers in the banquet; Beowulf is my name.
I shall gladly set out to the son of Healfdene,
most famous of kings, the cause of my journey,
lay it before your lord, if he will allow us kindly
to greet in person his most gracious self.'

Then Wulfgar spoke; the warlike spirit
of this Wendel prince, his wisdom in judgement,
were known to many. 'The Master of the Danes,
Lord of the Scyldings, shall learn of your request.
I shall gladly ask my honoured chief,
giver of arm-bands, about your undertaking,
and soon bear the answer back again to you
that my gracious lord shall think good to make.'

He strode rapidly to the seat of Hrothgar,
old and grey-haired among the guard of earls,
stepped forward briskly, stood before the shoulders

of the King of the Danes; a court's ways were known
   to him.
Then Wulfgar addressed his dear master:
'Men have come here from the country of the Geats,
borne from afar over the back of the sea;
these battle-companions call the man
who leads them, Beowulf. The boon they ask
is, my lord, that they may hold
converse with you. Do not, kind Hrothgar,
refuse them audience in the answer you vouchsafe;
accoutrement would clearly bespeak them
of earls' rank. Indeed the leader
who guided them here seems of great account.'

The Guardian of the Scyldings gave his answer:
'I knew him when he was a child!
It was to his old father, Edgetheow, that
Hrethel the Geat gave in marriage
his one daughter. Well does the son
now pay this call on a proven ally!

   The seafarers used to say, I remember,
who took our gifts to the Geat people
in token of friendship—that this fighting man
in his hand's grasp had the strength
of thirty other men. I am thinking that

the Holy God, as a grace to us
Danes in the West, has directed him here
against Grendel's oppression. This good man shall be
offered treasures in return for his courage.

Waste no time now but tell them to come in
that they may see this company seated together;
make sure to say that they are most welcome
to the people of the Danes.'
                                    Promptly Wulfgar
turned to the doors and told his message:
'The Master of Battles bids me announce,
the Lord of the North Danes, that he knows your
    ancestry;
I am to tell you all, determined venturers
over the seas, that you are sure of welcome.
You may go in now in your gear of battle,
set eyes on Hrothgar, helmed as you are.
But battle-shafts and shields of linden wood
may here await your words' outcome.'

The prince arose, around him warriors
in dense escort; detailed by the chief,
a group remained to guard the weapons.
The Geats swung in behind their stout leader
over Heorot's floor. The hero led on,

hard under helmet, to the hearth, where he stopped.
Then Beowulf spoke; bent by smith's skill
the meshed rings of his mailshirt glittered.
'Health to Hrothgar! I am Hygelac's kinsman
and serve in his fellowship. Fame-winning deeds
have come early to my hands. The affair of Grendel
has been made known to me on my native turf.
The sailors speak of this splendid hall,
this most stately building, standing idle
and silent of voices, as soon as the evening light
has hidden below the heaven's bright edge.
Whereupon it was urged by the ablest men
among our people, men proved in counsel,
that I should seek you out, most sovereign Hrothgar.
These men knew well the weight of my hands.
Had they not seen me come home from fights
where I had bound five Giants—their blood was upon
    me—
cleaned out a nest of them? Had I not crushed on the
    wave
sea-serpents by night in narrow struggle,
broken the beasts? (The bane of the Geats,
they had asked for their trouble.) And shall *I* not try
a single match with this monster Grendel,
a trial against this troll?

                                   To you I will now
put one request, Royal Scylding,
Shield of the South Danes, one sole favour
that you'll not deny me, dear lord of your people,
now that I have come thus far, Fastness of Warriors;
that I alone may be allowed, with my loyal and
    determined
crew of companions, to cleanse your hall Heorot.

        As I am informed that this unlovely one
is careless enough to carry no weapon,
so that my lord Hygelac, my leader in war,
may take joy in me, I abjure utterly
the bearing of sword or shielding yellow
board in this battle! With bare hands shall I
grapple with the fiend, fight to the death here,
hater and hated! He who is chosen
shall deliver himself to the Lord's judgement.

        If he can contrive it, we may count upon Grendel
to eat quite fearlessly the flesh of Geats
here in this war-hall; has he not chewed
on the strength of this nation? There will be no need,
    Sir,
for you to bury my head; he will have me gladly,
if death should take me, though darkened with blood.

He will bear my bloody corpse away, bent on eating it,
make his meal alone, without misgiving,
bespatter his moor-lair. The disposing of my body
need occupy you no further then.
But if the fight should take me, you would forward to
   Hygelac
this best of battle-shirts, that my breast now wears.
The queen of war-coats, it is the bequest of Hrethel
and from the forge of Wayland. Fate will take its
   course!'

Then Hrothgar spoke, the Helmet of the Scyldings:
'So it is to fight in our defence, my friend Beowulf,
and as an office of kindness that you have come to us
   here!
Great was the feud that your father set off
when his hand struck down Heatholaf in death
among the Wylfings. The Weather-Geats
did not dare to keep him then, for dread of war,
and he left them to seek out the South-Danish
   folk,
the glorious Scyldings, across the shock of waters.
I had assumed sway over the Scylding nation
and in my youth ruled this rich kingdom,
storehouse of heroes. Heorogar was then dead,
the son of Healfdene had hastened from us,

my elder brother; a better man than I!
I then settled the feud with fitting payment,
sent to the Wylfings over the water's back
old things of beauty; against which I'd the oath of your
  father.

It is a sorrow in spirit for me to say to any man
—a grief in my heart—what the hatred of Grendel
has brought me to in Heorot, what humiliation,
what harrowing pain. My hall-companions,
my war-band, are dwindled; Weird has swept them
into the power of Grendel. Yet God could easily
check the ravages of this reckless fiend!
They often boasted, when the beer was drunk,
and called out over the ale-cup, my captains in battle,
that they would here await, in this wassailing-place,
with deadliness of iron edges, the onset of Grendel.
When morning brought the bright daylight
this mead-hall was seen all stained with blood:
blood had soaked its shining floor,
it was a house of slaughter. More slender grew my
strength of dear warriors; death took them off. . . .
Yet sit now to the banquet, where you may soon
  attend,
should the mood so take you, some tale of victory.'

A bench was then cleared for the company of Geats
there in the beer-hall, for the whole band together.
The stout-hearted warriors went to their places,
bore their strength proudly. Prompt in his office,
the man who held the horn of bright mead
poured out its sweetness. The song of the poet
again rang in Heorot. The heroes laughed loud
in the great gathering of the Geats and the Danes.

Then *Unferth* spoke, the son of Edgelaf,
sitting at the feet of the Father of the Scyldings,
unbound a battle-rune. Beowulf's undertaking,
the seaman's bold venture, vexed him much.
He could not allow that another man
should hold under heaven a higher title
to wonders in the world than went with his own name.
'Is this the Beowulf of Breca's swimming-match,
who strove against him on the stretched ocean,
when for pride the pair of you proved the seas
and for a trite boast entrusted your lives
to the deep waters, undissuadable
by effort of friend or foe whatsoever
from that swimming on the sea? A sorry contest!
Your arms embraced the ocean's streams,
you beat the wave-way, wove your hand-movements,

and danced on the Spear-Man. The sea boiled with
    whelming
waves of winter; in the water's power
you laboured seven nights: and then you *lost* your
    swimming-match,
his might was the greater; morning found him
cast by the sea on the coast of the Battle-Reams.
He made his way back to the marches of the
    Brondings,
to his father-land, friend to his people,
and to the city-fastness where he had subjects,
    treasure
and his own stronghold. The son of Beanstan
performed to the letter what he had promised to you.
I see little hope then of a happier outcome
—though in other conflicts elsewhere in the world
you may indeed have prospered—if you propose
    awaiting
Grendel all night, on his own ground, unarmed.'

Then spoke Beowulf, son of Edgetheow:
'I thank my friend Unferth, who unlocks us this tale
of Breca's bragged exploit; the beer lends
eloquence to his tongue. But the truth is as I've said:
I had more sea-strength, outstaying Breca's,
and endured underwater a much worse struggle.

It was in early manhood that we undertook
with a public boast—both of us still
very young men—to venture our lives
on the open ocean; which we accordingly did.
Hard in our right hands we held each a sword
as we went through the sea, so to keep off
the whales from us. If he whitened the ocean,
no wider appeared the water between us.
He could not away from me; nor would I from him.
Thus stroke for stroke we stitched the ocean
five nights and days, drawn apart then
by cold storm on the cauldron of waters:
under lowering night the northern wind
fell on us in warspite: the waves were rough!

    The unfriendliness was then aroused of the fishes
  of the deep.
Against sea-beasts my body-armour,
hand-linked and hammered, helped me then,
this forge-knot battleshirt bright with gold,
decking my breast. Down to the bottom
I was plucked in rage by this reptile-fish,
pinned in his grip. But I got the chance
to thrust once at the ugly creature
with my weapon's point: war took off then
the mighty monster; mine was the hand did it.

Then loathsome snouts snickered by me,
swarmed at my throat. I served them out
with my good sword, gave them what they asked for:
those scaly flesh-eaters sat not down
to dine on Beowulf, they browsed not on me
in that picnic they'd designed in the dingles of the sea.
Daylight found them dispersed instead
up along the beaches where my blade had laid them
soundly asleep; since then they have never
troubled the passage of travellers over
that deep water-way. Day in the east grew,
God's bright beacon, and the billows sank
so that I then could see the headlands,
the windy cliffs. "Weird saves oft
the man undoomed if he undaunted be!"—
and it was my part then to put to the sword
seven sea-monsters, in the severest fight
by night I have heard of under heaven's vault;
a man more sorely pressed the seas never held.
I came with my life from the compass of my foes,
but tired from the struggle. The tide bore me
away on its currents to the coasts of the Lapps,
whelms of water.

        No whisper has yet reached me
of sword-ambushes survived, nor such scathing perils
in connection with your name! Never has Breca,

nor you Unferth either, in open battle-play
framed such a deed of daring with your
shining swords—small as my action was.
You have killed only kindred, kept your blade
for those closest in blood; you're a clever man,
  Unferth,
but you'll endure hell's damnation for that.

It speaks for itself, my son of Edgelaf,
that Grendel had never grown such a terror,
this demon had never dealt your lord
such havoc in Heorot, had your heart's intention
been so grim for battle as you give us to believe.
He's learnt there's in fact not the least need
excessively to respect the spite of this people,
the scathing steel-thresh of the Scylding nation.
He spares not a single sprig of your Danes
in extorting his tribute, but treats himself proud,
butchering and dispatching, and expects no resistance
from the spear-wielding Scyldings.
                              I'll show him Geatish
strength and stubbornness shortly enough now,
a lesson in war. He who wishes shall go then
blithe to the banquet when the breaking light
of another day shall dawn for men
and the sun shine glorious in the southern sky.'

Great then was the hope of the grey-locked Hrothgar,
warrior, giver of rings. Great was the trust
of the Shield of the Danes, shepherd of the people,
attending to Beowulf's determined resolve.

There was laughter of heroes, harp-music ran,
words were warm-hearted. *Wealhtheow* moved,
mindful of courtesies, the queen of Hrothgar,
glittering to greet the Geats in the hall,
peerless lady; but to the land's guardian
she offered first the flowing cup,
bade him be blithe at the beer-drinking,
gracious to his people; gladly the conqueror
partook of the banquet, tasted the hall-cup.
The Helming princess then passed about among
the old and the young men in each part of the hall,
bringing the treasure-cup, until the time came
when the flashing-armed queen, complete in all virtues,
carried out to Beowulf the brimming vessel;
she greeted the Geat, and gave thanks to the Lord
in words wisely chosen, her wish being granted
to meet with a man who might be counted on
for aid against these troubles. He took then the cup,
a man violent in war, at Wealhtheow's hand,
and framed his utterance, eager for the conflict.

Thus spoke Beowulf son of Edgetheow:
'This was my determination in taking to the ocean,
benched in the ship among my band of fellows,
that I should once and for all accomplish the wishes
of your adopted people, or pass to the slaughter,
viced in my foe's grip. This vow I shall accomplish,
a deed worthy of an earl; decided otherwise
here in this mead-hall to meet my ending-day!'

This speech sounded sweet to the lady,
the vaunt of the Geat; glittering she moved
to her lord's side, splendid folk-queen.

Then at last Heorot heard once more
words of courage, the carousing of a people
singing their victories; till the son of Healfdene
desired at length to leave the feast,
be away to his night's rest; aware of the monster
brooding his attack on the tall-gabled hall
from the time they had seen the sun's lightness
to the time when darkness drowns everything
and under its shadow-cover shapes do glide
dark beneath the clouds. The company came to its feet.

Then did the heroes, Hrothgar and Beowulf,
salute each other; success he wished him,

control of the wine-hall, and with this word left him:
'Never since I took up targe and sword
have I at any instance to any man beside,
thus handed over Heorot, as I here do to you.
Have and hold now the house of the Danes!
Bend your mind and your body to this task
and wake against the foe! There'll be no want of
   liberality
if you come out alive from this ordeal of courage.'
Then Hrothgar departed, the Protector of the Danes
passed from the hall at the head of his troop.
The war-leader sought Wealhtheow his queen,
the companion of his bed.

                     Thus did the King of Glory,
to oppose this Grendel, appoint a hall-guard
—so the tale went abroad—who took on a special
task at the court—to cope with the monster.
The Geat prince placed all his trust
in his mighty strength, his Maker's favour.

He now uncased himself of his coat of mail,
unhelmed his head, handed his attendant
his embellished sword, best of weapons,
and bade him take care of these trappings of
   war.
Beowulf then made a boasting speech,

the Geat man, before mounting his bed:
'I fancy my fighting-strength, my performance in
  combat,
at least as greatly as Grendel does his;
and therefore I shall not cut short his life
with a slashing sword—too simple a business.
He has not the art to answer me in kind,
hew at my shield, shrewd though he be
at his nasty catches. No, we'll at night play
without any weapons—if unweaponed he dare
to face me in fight. The Father in His wisdom
shall apportion the honours then, the All-holy Lord,
to whichever side shall seem to Him fit.'

Then the hero lay down, leant his head
on the bolster there; about him many
brave sea-warriors bowed to their hall-rest.
Not one of them thought he would thence be departing
ever to set eyes on his own country,
the home that nourished him, or its noble people;
for they had heard how many men of the Danes
death had dragged from that drinking-hall.
But God was to grant to the Geat people
the clue to war-success in the web of fate—
His help and support; so that they all did
overcome the foe—through the force of one

unweaponed man. The Almighty Lord
has ruled the affairs of the race of men
thus from the beginning.

          Gliding through the shadows came
the walker in the night; the warriors slept
whose task was to hold the horned building,
all except one. It was well-known to men
that the demon could not drag them to the shades
without God's willing it; yet the one man kept
unblinking watch. He awaited, heart swelling
with anger against his foe, the ordeal of battle.
Down off the moorlands' misting fells came
Grendel stalking; God's brand was on him.
The spoiler meant to snatch away
from the high hall some of human race.
He came on under the clouds, clearly saw at last
the gold-hall of men, the mead-drinking place
nailed with gold plates. That was not the first visit
he had paid to the hall of Hrothgar the Dane:
he never before and never after
harder luck nor hall-guards found.

Walking to the hall came this warlike creature
condemned to agony. The door gave way,
toughened with iron, at the touch of those hands.
Rage-inflamed wreckage-bent, he ripped open

the jaws of the hall. Hastening on,
the foe then stepped onto the unstained floor,
angrily advanced: out of his eyes stood
an unlovely light like that of fire.
He saw then in the hall a host of young soldiers,
a company of kinsmen caught away in sleep,
a whole warrior-band. In his heart he laughed then,
horrible monster, his hopes swelling
to a gluttonous meal. He meant to wrench
the life from each body that lay in the place
before night was done. It was not to be;
he was no longer to feast on the flesh of mankind
after that night.

      Narrowly the powerful
kinsman of Hygelac kept watch how the ravager
set to work with his sudden catches;
nor did the monster mean to hang back.
As a first step he set his hands on
a sleeping soldier, savagely tore at him,
gnashed at his bone-joints, bolted huge gobbets,
sucked at his veins, and had soon eaten
all of the dead man, even down to his
hands and feet.

      Forward he stepped,
stretched out his hands to seize the warrior
calmly at rest there, reached out for him with his

unfriendly fingers: but the faster man
forestalling, sat up, sent back his arm.
The upholder of evils at once knew
he had not met, on middle earth's
extremest acres, with any man
of harder hand-grip: his heart panicked.
He was quit of the place no more quickly for that.

Eager to be away, he ailed for his darkness
and the company of devils; the dealings he had there
were like nothing he had come across in his lifetime.
Then Hygelac's brave kinsman called to mind
that evening's utterance, upright he stood,
fastened his hold till fingers were bursting.
The monster strained away: the man stepped closer.
The monster's desire was for darkness between them,
direction regardless, to get out and run
for his fen-bordered lair; he felt his grip's strength
crushed by his enemy. It was an ill journey
the rough marauder had made to Heorot.

The crash in the banqueting-hall came to the Danes,
the men of the guard that remained in the building,
with the taste of death. The deepening rage
of the claimants to Heorot caused it to resound.
It was indeed wonderful that the wine-supper-hall

withstood the wrestling pair, that the world's palace
fell not to the ground. But it was girt firmly,
both inside and out, by iron braces
of skilled manufacture. Many a figured
gold-worked wine-bench, as we heard it,
started from the floor at the struggles of that pair.
The men of the Danes had not imagined that
any of mankind by what method soever
might undo that intricate, antlered hall,
sunder it by strength—unless it were swallowed up in
the embraces of fire.
                Fear entered into
the listening North Danes, as that noise rose up again
strange and strident. It shrilled terror
to the ears that heard it through the hall's side-wall,
the grisly plaint of God's enemy,
his song of ill-success, the sobs of the damned one
bewailing his pain. He was pinioned there
by the man of all mankind living
in this world's estate the strongest of his hands.

Not for anything would the earls' guardian
let his deadly guest go living:
he did not count his continued existence
of the least use to anyone. The earls ran
to defend the person of their famous prince;

they drew their ancestral swords to bring
what aid they could to their captain, Beowulf.
They were ignorant of this, when they entered the
   fight,
boldly-intentioned battle-friends,
to hew at Grendel, hunt his life
on every side—that no sword on earth,
not the truest steel, could touch their assailant;
for by a spell he had dispossessed all
blades of their bite on him.
                A bitter parting
from life was that day destined for him;
the eldritch spirit was sent off on his
far faring into the fiends' domain.

It was then that this monster, who, moved by spite
against human kind, had caused so much harm
—so feuding with God—found at last
that flesh and bone were to fail him in the end;
for Hygelac's great-hearted kinsman
had him by the hand; and hateful to each
was the breath of the other.
                A breach in the giant
flesh-frame showed then, shoulder-muscles
sprang apart, there was a snapping of tendons,
bone-locks burst. To Beowulf the glory

of this fight was granted; Grendel's lot
to flee the slopes fen-ward with flagging heart,
to a den where he knew there could be no relief,
no refuge for a life at its very last stage,
whose surrender-day had dawned. The Danish hopes
in this fatal fight had found their answer.

He had cleansed Heorot. He who had come from afar,
deep-minded, strong-hearted, had saved the hall
from persecution. He was pleased with his night's
     work,
the deed he had done. Before the Danish people
the Geat captain had made good his boast,
had taken away all their unhappiness,
the evil menace under which they had lived,
enduring it by dire constraint,
no slight affliction. As a signal to all
the hero hung up the hand, the arm
and torn-off shoulder, the entire limb,
Grendel's whole grip, below the gable of the roof.

There was, as I heard it, at hall next morning
a great gathering in the gift-hall yard
to see the wonder. Along the wide highroads
the chiefs of the clans came from near and far
to see the foe's footprints. It may fairly be said

that his parting from life aroused no pity in any
who tracked the spoor-blood of his blind flight
for the monster's mere-pool; with mood flagging
and strength crushed, he had staggered onwards;
each step evidenced his ebbing life's blood.

The tarn was troubled; a terrible wave-thrash
brimmed it, bubbling; black-mingled,
the warm wound-blood welled upwards.
He had dived to his doom, he had died miserably;
here in his fen-lair he had laid aside
his heathen soul. Hell welcomed it.
Then the older retainers turned back on the way
journeyed with much joy; joined by the young men,
the warriors on white horses wheeled away from the
     mere
in bold mood. Beowulf's feat
was much spoken of, and many said,
that between the seas, south or north,
over earth's stretch no other man
beneath the sky's shifting excelled Beowulf,
of all who wielded the sword he was worthiest to
     rule.
In saying this they did not slight in the least
the gracious Hrothgar, for he was a good king.

Where, as they went, their way broadened
they would match their mounts, making them leap
along the best stretches, the strife-eager
on their fallow horses. Or a fellow of the king's,
whose head was a storehouse of the storied verse,
whose tongue gave gold to the language
of the treasured repertory, wrought a new lay
made in the measure. The man struck up,
found the phrase, framed rightly
the deed of Beowulf, drove the tale,
rang word-changes.

       Of Wæls's great son,
Sigemund, he spoke then, spelling out to them
all he had heard of that hero's strife,
his fights, strange feats, far wanderings,
the feuds and the blood split. Fitela alone heard
these things not well nor widely known to men,
when Sigemund chose to speak in this vein
to his sister's son. They were inseparable
in every fight, the firmest of allies;
their swords had between them scythed to the ground
a whole race of monsters. The reputation
that spread at his death was no slight one:
Sigemund it was who had slain the dragon,
the keeper of the hoard; the king's son walked
under the grey rock, he risked alone

that fearful conflict; Fitela was not there.
Yet it turned out well for him, his weapon transfixed
the marvellous snake, struck in the cave-wall,
best of swords; the serpent was dead.
Sigemund's valour had so prevailed
that the whole ring-hoard was his to enjoy
dispose of as he wished. Wæls's great son
loaded his ship with shining trophies,
stacking them by the mast; the monster shrivelled
    away.

He was by far the most famous of adventurers
among the peoples, this protector of warriors,
for the deeds by which he had distinguished himself.
Heremod's stature and strength had decayed then,
his daring diminished. Deeply betrayed
into the fiends' power, far among the Giants
he was dispatched to death. Dark sorrows
drove him mad at last. A deadly grief
he had become to his people and the princes of his
    land.
Wise men among the leaders had lamented that career,
their fierce one's fall, who in former days
had looked to him for relief of their ills,
hoping that their lord's son would live and in ripeness
assume the kingdom, the care of his people,

the hoard and the stronghold, the storehouse of heroes,
the Scylding homeland. Whereas Hygelac's kinsman
endeared himself ever more deeply to friends
and to all mankind, evil seized Heremod.

The riders returning came racing their horses
along dusty-pale roads. The dawn had grown
into broadest day, and, drawn by their eagerness
to see the strange sight, there had assembled at the
    hall
many keen warriors. The king himself,
esteemed for excellence, stepped glorious
from his wife's chambers, the warden of ring-hoards,
with much company; and his queen walked
the mead-path by him, her maidens following.

Taking his stand on the steps of the hall,
Hrothgar beheld the hand of Grendel
below the gold gable-end; and gave speech:
'Let swift thanks be given to the Governor of All,
seeing this sight! I have suffered a thousand
spites from Grendel: but God works ever
miracle upon miracle, the Master of Heaven.
Until yesterday I doubted whether
our afflictions would find a remedy
in my lifetime, since this loveliest of halls

stood slaughter-painted, spattered with blood.
For all my counsellors this was a cruel sorrow,
for none of them imagined they could mount a defence
of the Scylding stronghold against such enemies,
warlocks, demons!

                But one man has,
by the Lord's power, performed the thing
that all our thought and arts to this day
had failed to do. She may indeed say,
whoever she be that brought into the world
this young man here—if yet she lives—
that the God of Old was gracious to her
in her child-bearing. Beowulf, I now take you
to my bosom as a son, O best of men,
and cherish you in my heart. Hold yourself well
in this new relation! You will lack for nothing
that lies in my gift of the goods of this world:
lesser offices have elicited reward,
we have honoured from our hoard less heroic
    men,
far weaker in war. But you have well ensured
by the deeds of your hands an undying honour
for your name for ever. May the Almighty Father
yield you always the success that you yesternight
    enjoyed!'

Beowulf spoke, son of Edgetheow:
'We willingly undertook this test of courage,
risked a match with the might of the stranger,
and performed it all. I would prefer, though,
that you had rather seen the rest of him here,
the whole length of him, lying here dead.
I had meant to catch him, clamp him down
with a cruel lock to his last resting-place;
with my hands upon him, I would have him
   soon
in the throes of death—unless he disappeared!
But I had not a good enough grip to prevent
his getting away, when God did not wish it;
the fiend in his flight was far too violent,
my life's enemy. But he left his hand
behind him here, so as to have his life,
and his arm and shoulder. And all for nothing:
it brought him no respite, wretched creature.
He lives no longer, laden with sins,
to plague mankind: pain has set
heavy hands on him, and hasped about him
fatal fetters. He is forced to await now,
like a guilty criminal, a greater judgement,
where the Lord in His splendour shall pass sentence
   upon him.'

The son of Edgelaf was more silent then
in boasting of his own battle-deeds:
the athelings gazed at what the earl's strength
had hung there—the hand, high up under the roof,
and the fingers of their foe. From the front, each one
of the nail-sockets seemed steel to the eye,
each spur on the hand of that heathen warrior
was a terrible talon. They told each other
nothing could be hard enough to harm it at all,
not the most ancient of iron swords
would bite on that bloody battle-hand.

Other hands were then pressed to prepare the inside
of the banqueting-hall, and briskly too.
Many were ready, both men and women,
to adorn the guest-hall. Gold-embroidered tapestries
glowed from the walls, with wonderful sights
for every creature that cared to look at them.
The bright building had badly started
in all its inner parts, despite its iron bands,
and the hinges were ripped off. Only the roof survived
unmarred and in one piece when the monstrous one,
flecked with his crimes, had fled the place
in despair of his life.
                              But to elude death
is not easy: attempt it who will,

he shall go to the place prepared for each
of the sons of men, the soul-bearers
dwelling on earth, ordained them by fate:
laid fast in that bed, the body shall sleep
when the feast is done.

                    In due season
the king himself came to the hall;
Healfdene's son would sit at the banquet.
No people has gathered in greater retinue,
borne themselves better about their ring-giver.
Men known for their courage came to the benches,
rejoiced in the feast; they refreshed themselves
    kindly
with many a mead-cup; in their midst the brave
    kinsmen,
father's brother and brother's son,
Hrothgar and Hrothulf. Heorot's floor was
filled with friends: falsity in those days
had no place in the dealings of the Danish people.

Then as a sign of victory the son of Healfdene
bestowed on Beowulf a standard worked in gold,
a figured battle-banner, breast and head-armour;
and many admired the marvellous sword
that was borne before the hero. Beowulf drank with

the company in the hall. He had no cause to be
    ashamed of
gifts so fine before the fighting-men!
I have not heard that many men at arms
have given four such gifts of treasure
more openly to another at the mead.
At the crown of the helmet, the head-protector,
was a rim, with wire wound round it, to stop
the file-hardened blade that fights have tempered
from shattering it, when the shield-warrior
must go out against grim enemies.

The king then ordered eight war-horses
with glancing bridles to be brought within walls
and onto the floor. Fretted with gold
and studded with stones was one saddle there!
This was the battle-seat of the Bulwark of the Danes,
when in the sword-play the son of Healfdene
would take his part; the prowess of the king
had never failed at the front where the fighting was
    mortal.
The Protector of the Sons of Scyld then gave
both to Beowulf, bidding him take care
to use them well, both weapons and horses.
Thus did the glorious prince, guardian of the treasure,
reward these deeds, with both war-horses and armour;

of such open-handedness no honest man
could ever speak in disparagement.

Then the lord of men also made a gift
of treasure to each who had adventured with Beowulf
over the sea's paths, seated now at the benches—
an old thing of beauty. He bade compensation
to be made too, in gold, for the man whom Grendel
had horribly murdered; more would have gone
had not the God overseeing us, and the resolve of a
    man,
stood against this Weird. The Wielder guided then
the dealings of mankind, as He does even now.
A mind that seeks to understand and grasp this
is therefore best. Both bad and good,
and much of both, must be borne in a lifetime
spent on this earth in these anxious days.

Then string and song sounded together
before Healfdene's Helper-in-battle:
the lute was taken up and tales recited
when Hrothgar's bard was bidden to sing
a hall-song for the men on the mead-benches.
It was how disaster came to the songs of *Finn*:
first the Half-Dane champion, *Hnæf* of the Scyldings,
was fated to fall in the Frisian ambush.

Hildeburgh their lady had little cause to speak
of the good faith of the Jutes; guiltless she had suffered
in that linden-wood clash the loss of her closest ones,
her son and her brother, both born to die there,
struck down by the spear. Sorrowful princess!
This decree of fate the daughter of Hoc
mourned with good reason; for when morning came
the clearness of heaven disclosed to her
the murder of those kindred who were the cause of all
her earthly bliss.

                Battle had also claimed
all but a few of Finn's retainers
in that place of assembly; he was unable therefore
to bring to a finish the fight with *Hengest*,
force out and crush the few survivors
of Hnæf's troop. The truce-terms they put to him
were that he should make over a mead-hall to the
  Danes,
with high-seat and floor; half of it
to be held by them, half by the Jutes.
In sharing out goods, that the son of Folcwalda
should every day give honour to the Danes
of Hengest's party, providing rings
and prizes from the hoard, plated with gold,
treating them identically in the drinking-hall
as when he chose to cheer his own Frisians.

On both sides they then bound themselves fast
in a pact of friendship. Finn then swore
strong unexceptioned oaths to Hengest
to hold in honour, as advised by his counsellors,
the battle-survivors; similarly no man
by word or deed to undo the pact,
as by mischievous cunning to make complaint of it,
despite that they were serving the slayer of their prince,
since their lordless state so constrained them to do;
but that if any Frisian should fetch the feud to mind
and by taunting words awaken the bad blood,
it should be for the sword's edge to settle it then.

The pyre was erected, the ruddy gold
brought from the hoard, and the best warrior
of Scylding race was ready for the burning.
Displayed on his pyre, plain to see
were the bloody mail-shirt, the boars on the helmets,
iron-hard, gold-clad; and gallant men about him
all marred by their wounds; mighty men had fallen
    there.
Hildeburgh then ordered her own son
to be given to the funeral fire of Hnæf
for the burning of his bones; bade him be laid
at his uncle's side. She sang the dirges,
bewailed her grief. The warrior went up;

the greatest of corpse-fires coiled to the sky,
roared before the mounds. There were melting heads
and bursting wounds, as the blood sprang out
from weapon-bitten bodies. Blazing fire,
most insatiable of spirits, swallowed the remains
of the victims of both nations. Their valour was no
   more.

The warriors then scattered and went to their homes.
Missing their comrades, they made for Friesland,
the home and high stronghold. But Hengest still,
as he was constrained to do, stayed with Finn
a death-darkened winter in dreams of his homeland.
He was prevented from passage of the sea
in his ring-beaked boat: the boiling ocean
fought with the wind; winter locked the seas
in his icy binding; until another year
came at last to the dwellings, as it does still,
continually keeping its season,
the weather of rainbows.

                 Now winter had fled
and earth's breast was fair, the exile strained
to leave these lodgings; yet it was less the voyage
that exercised his mind than the means of his
   vengeance,
the bringing about of the bitter conflict

that he meditated for the men of the Jutes.
So he did not decline the accustomed remedy,
when the son of Hunlaf set across his knees
that best of blades, his battle-gleaming sword;
the Giants were acquainted with the edges of that
    steel.

And so, in his hall, at the hands of his enemies,
Finn received the fatal sword-thrust;
Guthlaf and Oslaf, after the sea-crossing,
proclaimed their tribulations, their treacherous
    entertainment,
and named the author of them; anger in the breast
rose irresistible. Red was the hall then
with the lives of foemen. Finn was slain there,
the king among his troop, and the queen taken.
The Scylding crewmen carried to the ship
the hall-furnishings of Friesland's king,
all they could find at Finnsburgh
in gemstones and jewelwork. Journeying back,
they returned to the Danes their true-born lady,
restored her to her people.

               Thus the story was sung,
the gleeman's lay. Gladness mounted,
bench-mirth rang out, the bearers gave

wine from wonderful vessels. Then came Wealhtheow
  forward,
going with golden crown to where the great heroes
were sitting, uncle and nephew; their bond was sound
  at that time,
each was true to the other. Likewise Unferth the
  spokesman
sat at the footstool of Hrothgar. All had faith in his
  spirit,
accounted his courage great—though toward his
  kinsmen he had not been
kind at the clash of swords.

The Scylding queen then spoke:

'Accept this cup, my king and lord,
giver of treasure. Let your gaiety be shown,
gold-friend of warriors, and to the Geats speak
in words of friendship, for this well becomes a man.
Be gracious to these Geats, and let the gifts you have
  had
from near and far, not be forgotten now.

I hear it is your wish to hold this warrior
henceforward as your son. Heorot is cleansed,
the ring-hall bright again: therefore bestow while you
  may

these blessings liberally, and leave to your kinsmen
the land and its people when your passing is
    decreed,
your meeting with fate. For may I not count
on my gracious Hrothulf to guard honourably
our young ones here, if you, my lord,
should give over this world earlier than he?
I am sure that he will show to our children
answerable kindness, if he keeps in remembrance
all that we have done to indulge and advance
    him,
the honours we bestowed on him when he was still a
    child.'

Then she turned to the bench where her boys were
    sitting,
Hrethric and Hrothmund, among the heroes' sons,
young men together; where the good man sat also
between the two brothers, Beowulf the Geat.
Then the cup was taken to him and he was entreated
    kindly
to honour their feast; ornate gold
was presented in trophy: two arm-wreaths,
with robes and rings also, and the richest collar
I have ever heard of in all the world.

Never under heaven have I heard of a finer
prize among heroes—since Hama carried off
the Brising necklace to his bright city,
that gold-cased jewel; he gave the slip
to the machinations of Eormenric, and made his name
  forever.

This gold was to be on the neck of the grandson of
  Swerting
on the last of his harryings, Hygelac the Geat,
as he stood before the standard astride his plunder,
defending his war-haul: Weird struck him down;
in his superb pride he provoked disaster
in the Frisian feud. This fabled collar
the great war-king wore when he crossed
the foaming waters; he fell beneath his shield.
The king's person passed into Frankish hands,
together with his corselet, and this collar also.
They were lesser men that looted the slain;
for when the carnage was over, the corpse-field was
  littered
with the people of the Geats.

       Applause filled the hall;
then Wealhtheow spoke, and her words were
  attended.

'Take pride in this jewel, have joy of this mantle
drawn from our treasuries, most dear Beowulf!
May fortune come with them and may you flourish in
   your youth!
Proclaim your strength; but in counsel to these boys
be a gentle guardian, and my gratitude will be seen.
Already you have so managed that men everywhere
will hold you in honour for all time,
even to the cliffs at the world's end, washed by Ocean,
the wind's range. All the rest of your life
must be happy, prince; and prosperity I wish you too,
abundance of treasure! But be to my son
a friend in deed, most favoured of men.
You see how open is each earl here with his neighbour,
temperate of heart, and true to his lord.
The nobles are loyal, the lesser people dutiful;
wine mellows the men to move to my bidding.'

She walked back to her place. What a banquet that
   was!
The men drank their wine: the weird they did not
   know,
destined from of old, the doom that was to fall
on many of the earls there. When evening came
Hrothgar departed to his private bower,
the king to his couch; countless were the men

who watched over the hall, as they had often done
  before.
They cleared away the benches, and covered the
  floor
with beds and bolsters: the best at the feast
bent to his hall-rest, hurried to his doom.
Each by his head placed his polished shield,
the lindens of battle. On the benches aloft,
above each atheling, easily to be seen,
were the ring-stitched mail-coat, the mighty helmet
steepling above the fray, and the stout spear-shaft.
It was their habit always, at home or on campaign,
to be ready for war, in whichever case,
whatsoever the hour might be
that the need came on their lord: what a nation they
  were!

Then they sank into sleep. A savage penalty
one paid for his night's rest! It was no new thing for
  that people
since Grendel had settled in the gold-giving hall,
working his evil, until the end came,
death for his misdeeds. It was declared then to men,
and received by every ear, that for all this time
a survivor had been living, an avenger for their foe
and his grim life's-leaving: *Grendel's Mother* herself,

a monstrous ogress, was ailing for her loss.
She had been doomed to dwell in the dread waters,
in the chilling currents, because of that blow
whereby Cain became the killer of his brother,
his own father's son. He stole away, branded,
marked for his murder, from all that men delight in,
to inhabit the wastelands.

                    Hosts of the ill ones
sprang from his begetting; as Grendel, that hateful
accursed outcast, who encountered at Heorot
a watchful man, waiting for the fight.
The grim one fastened his grip upon him there,
but he remembered his mighty strength,
the gift that the Lord had so largely bestowed on him,
and, putting his faith in the favour of the Almighty
and His aid and comfort, he overcame the foe,
put down the hell-fiend. How humbling was that flight
when the miserable outcast crept to his dying-place!
Thus mankind's enemy. But his Mother now purposed
to set out at last—savage in her grief—
on that wrath-bearing visit of vengeance for her son.

She came down to Heorot, where the heroes of the
   Danes
slept about the hall. A sudden change

was that for the men there when the Mother of
    Grendel
found her way in among them—though the fury of her
    onslaught
was less frightful than his; as the force of a woman,
her onset in a fight, is less feared by men,
where the bound blade, beaten out by hammers,
cuts, with its sharp edges shining with blood,
through the boars that bristle above the foes' helmets!

Many a hard sword was snatched up in the hall
from its rack above the benches; the broad shield was
    raised,
held in the hand firm; helmet and corselet
lay there unheeded when the horror was on them.
She was all eager to be out of the place
now that she was discovered, and escape with her life.
She caught a man quickly, clutched him to herself,
one of the athelings, and was away to the fen.
This was the hero that Hrothgar loved better
than any on earth among his retinue,
destroyed thus as he slept; he was a strong warrior,
noted in battle. (Beowulf was not there:
separate lodging had been assigned that night,
after the treasure-giving, to the Geat champion.)
Heorot was in uproar; the hand had gone with her,

blood-stained, familiar.

                              And so a fresh sorrow
came again to those dwellings. It was an evil bargain,
with both parties compelled to barter
the lives of their dearest. What disturbance of spirit
for the wise king, the white-haired soldier,
hearing the news that the nearest of his thanes
was dead and gone, his dearest man!

Beowulf was soon summoned to the chamber,
victory-blest man. And that valiant warrior
came with his following—it was at first light—
captain of his company, to where the king waited
to see if by some means the Swayer of All
would work a turning into this tale of sorrow.
The man excellent in warfare walked across the hall
flanked by his escort—the floor-timbers boomed—
to make his addresses to the Danish lord,
the Guide of the Ingwine. He inquired of him whether
the night had been quiet, after a call so urgent.

Hrothgar spoke, the Helmet of the Scyldings:
'Do not ask about our welfare! Woe has returned
to the Danish people with the death of *Ashhere*,
the elder brother of Yrmenlaf.

He was my closest counsellor, he was keeper of my
    thoughts,
he stood at my shoulder when we struck for our lives
at the crashing together of companies of foot,
when blows rained on boar-crests. Men of birth and
    merit
all should be as Ashhere was!
A bloodthirsty monster has murdered him in Heorot,
a wandering demon; whither this terrible one,
glorying in her prey, glad of her meal,
has returned to, I know not. She has taken vengeance
for the previous night, when you put an end to Grendel
with forceful finger-grasp, and in a fierce manner,
because he had diminished and destroyed my people
for far too long. He fell in that struggle
and forfeited his life; but now is followed by another
most powerful ravager. Revenge is her motive,
and in furthering her son's feud she has gone far
    enough,
—or thanes may be found who will think it so;
in their breasts they will grieve for their giver of rings,
bitter at heart. For the hand is stilled
that would openly have granted your every desire,

    I have heard it said by subjects of mine
who live in the country, counsellors in this hall,

that they have seen such a pair
of huge wayfarers haunting the moors,
otherworldly ones; and one of them,
so far as they might make it out,
was in woman's shape; but the shape of a man,
though twisted, trod also the tracks of exile
—save that he was more huge than any human being.
The country people have called him from of old
by the name of Grendel; they know of no father for
    him,
nor whether there have been such beings before
among the monster-race.
                            Mysterious is the region
they live in—of wolf-fells, wind-picked moors
and treacherous fen-paths: a torrent of water
pours down dark cliffs and plunges into the earth,
an underground flood. It is not far from here,
in terms of miles, that the Mere lies,
overcast with dark, crag-rooted trees
that hang in groves hoary with frost.
An uncanny sight may be seen at night there
—the fire in the water! The wit of living men
is not enough to know its bottom.
The hart that roams the hearth, when hounds have
    pressed him
long and hard, may hide in the forest

his antlered head; but the hart will die there
sooner than swim and save his life;
he will sell it on the brink there, for it is not a safe
    place.
And the wind can stir up wicked storms there,
whipping the swirling waters up
till they climb the clouds and clog the air,
making the skies weep.
                        Our sole remedy
is to turn again to you. The treacherous country
where that creature of sin is to be sought out
is strange to you as yet: seek then if you dare!
I shall reward the deed, as I did before,
with wealthy gifts of wreathèd ore,
treasures from the hoard, if you return again.'

Beowulf spoke, son of Edgetheow:
'Bear your grief, wise one! It is better for a man
to avenge his friend than to refresh his sorrow.
As we must all expect to leave
our life on this earth, we must earn some renown,
if we can, before death; daring is the thing
for a fighting man to be remembered by.

    Let Denmark's lord arise, and we shall rapidly see
then

where this kinswoman of Grendel's has gone away to!
I can promise you this, that she'll not protect herself by
   hiding
in any fold of the field, in any forest of the mountain,
in any dingle of the sea, dive where she will!
For this day, therefore, endure all your woes
with the patience that I may expect of you.'

The ancient arose and offered thanks to God,
to the Lord Almighty, for what this man had spoken.
A steed with braided man was bridled then,
a horse for Hrothgar; the hero-patriarch
rode out shining; shieldbearers marched
in troop beside him. The trace of her going
on the woodland paths was plainly to be seen,
stepping onwards; straight across
the fog-bound moor she had fetched away there
the lifeless body of the best man
of all who kept the courts of Hrothgar.
The sons of men then made their way
up steep screes, by scant tracks
where only one might walk, by wall-faced cliffs,
through haunted fens—uninhabitable country.

Going on head with a handful of the
keener men to reconnoitre,

Beowulf suddenly saw where some ash-trees
hung above a hoary rock
—a cheerless wood! And the water beneath it
was turbid with blood; bitter distress
was to be endured by the Danes who were there,
a grief for the earls, for every thane
of the Friends of the Scyldings, when they found there
the head of Ashhere by the edge of the cliff.

The men beheld the blood on the water,
its warm upwellings. The war-horn sang
an eager battle-cry. The band of foot-soldiers,
sitting by the water, could see multitudes
of strange sea-drakes swerving through the depths,
and water-snakes lay on the ledges of the cliffs,
such serpents and wild beasts as will sally out
in middle morning to make havoc
in the seas where ships sail.
                                        Slithering away
at the bright phrases of the battle-horn,
they were swollen with anger. An arrow from the
bow of Beowulf broke the life's thread
of one wave-thrasher; wedged in his throat
the iron dart; with difficulty then
did he swim through the deep, until death took him.
They struck him as he swam, and straightaway,

with their boar-spears barbed and tanged;
gaffed and battered, he was brought to the cliff-top,
strange lurker of the waves. They looked with wonder
at their grisly guest!

                The Geat put on
the armour of a hero, unanxious for his life:
the manufacture of the mailed shirt,
figured and vast, that must venture in the deep,
made it such a bulwark to his bone-framed chest
that the savage attack of an incensed enemy
could do no harm to the heart within it.
His head was encircled by a silver helmet
that was to strike down through the swirl of water,
disturb the depths. Adorned with treasure,
clasped with royal bands, it was right as at first
when the weapon-smith had wonderfully made it,
so that no sword should afterward be able to cut
    through
the defending wild boars that faced about it.
Not least among these mighty aids
was the hilted sword that Hrothgar's spokesman,
Unferth, lent him in his hour of trial.
Hrunting was its name; unique and ancient,
its edge was iron, annealed in venom
and tempered in blood; in battle it never
failed any hero whose hand took it up

at his setting out on a stern adventure
for the house of foes. This was not the first time
that it had to do heroic work.

It would seem that the strapping son of Edgelaf
had forgotten the speech he had spoken earlier,
eloquent with wine, for he offered the weapon now
to the better swordsman; himself he would not go
beneath the spume to display his valour
and risk his life; he lost his reputation there
for nerve and action. With the other man
it was otherwise once he had armed himself for battle.

Beowulf spoke, son of Edgetheow:
'I am eager to begin, great son of Healfdene.
Remember well, then, my wise lord,
provider of gold, what we agreed once before,
that if in your service it should so happen
that I am sundered from life, that you would assume
   the place
of a father towards me when I was gone.
Now extend your protection to the troop of my
   companions,
my young fellows, if the fight should take me;
convey also the gifts that you have granted to me,
beloved Hrothgar, to my lord Hygelac.

For on seeing this gold, the Geat chieftain,
Hrethel's son, will perceive from its value
that I had met with magnificent patronage
from a giver of jewels and that I had joy of him.
Let Unferth have the blade that I inherited
—he is a widely-known man—this wave-patterned
    sword
of rare hardness. With Hrunting shall I
achieve this deed—or death shall take me!'

After these words the Weather-Geat prince
dived into the Mere—he did not care
to wait for an answer—and the waves closed over
the daring man. It was a day's space almost
before he could glimpse ground at the bottom.

The grim and greedy guardian of the flood,
keeping her hungry hundred-season watch,
discovered at once that one from above,
a human, had sounded the home of the monsters.
She felt for the man and fastened upon him
her terrible hooks; but no harm came thereby
to the hale body within—the harness so ringed him
that she could not drive her dire fingers
through the mesh of the mail-shirt masking his
    limbs.

When she came to the bottom she bore him to her lair,
the mere-wolf, pinioning the mail-clad prince.
Not all his courage could enable him
to draw his sword; but swarming through the water,
throngs of sea-beasts threw themselves upon him
with ripping tusks to tear his battle-coat,
tormenting monsters. Then the man found
that he was in some enemy hall
where there was no water to weigh upon him
and the power of the flood could not pluck him away,
sheltered by its roof: a shining light he saw,
a bright fire blazing clearly.

It was then that he saw the size of this water-hag,
damned thing of the deep. He dashed out his weapon,
not stinting the stroke, and with such strength and
   violence
that the circled sword screamed on her head
a strident battle-song. But the stranger saw
his battle-flame refuse to bite
or hurt her at all; the edge failed
its lord in his need. It had lived through many
hand-to-hand conflicts, and carved through the helmets
of fated men. This was the first time
that this rare treasure had betrayed its name.
Determined still, intent on fame,

the nephew of Hygelac renewed his courage.
Furious, the warrior flung it to the ground,
spiral-patterned, precious in its clasps,
stiff and steel-edged; his own strength would suffice
   him,
the might of his hands. A man must act so
when he means in a fight to frame himself
a long-lasting glory; it is not life he thinks of.

The Geat prince went for Grendel's mother,
seized her by the shoulder—he was not sorry to be
   fighting—
his mortal foe, and with mounting anger
the man hard in battle hurled her to the ground.
She promptly repaid this present of his
as her ruthless hands reached out for him;
and the strongest of fighting-men stumbled in his
   weariness,
the firmest of foot-warriors fell to the earth.
She was down on this guest of hers and had drawn her
   knife,
broad, burnished of edge; for her boy was to be
   avenged,
her only son. Overspreading his back,
the shirt of mail shielded his life then,
barred the entry to edge and point.

Edgetheow's son would have ended his venture
deep under ground there, the Geat fighter,
had not the battle-shirt then brought him aid,
his war-shirt of steel. And the wise Lord,
the holy God, gave out the victory;
the Ruler of the Heavens rightly settled it
as soon as the Geat regained his feet.

He saw among the armour there the sword to bring
    him victory,
a Giant-sword from former days: formidable were its
    edges,
a warrior's admiration. This wonder of its kind
was yet so enormous that no other man
would be equal to bearing it in battle-play
—it was a Giant's forge that had fashioned it so well.
The Scylding champion, shaking with war-rage,
caught it by its rich hilt, and, careless of his life,
brandished its circles, and brought it down in fury
to take her full and fairly across the neck,
breaking the bones; the blade sheared
through the death-doomed flesh. She fell to the ground;
the sword was gory; he was glad at the deed.

Light glowed out and illumined the chamber
with a clearness such as the candle of heaven

sheds in the sky. He scoured the dwelling
in single-minded anger, the servant of Hygelac;
with his weapon high, and, holding to it firmly,
he stalked by the wall. Nor was the steel useless yet
to that man of battle, for he meant soon enough
to settle with Grendel for those stealthy raids
—there had been many of them—he had made on the
     West-Danes;
far more often than on that first occasion
when he had killed Hrothgar's hearth-companions,
slew them as they slept, and in their sleep ate up
of the folk of Denmark fifteen good men,
carrying off another of them
in foul robbery. The fierce champion
now settled this up with him: he saw where Grendel
lay at rest, limp from the fight;
his life had wasted through the wound he had got
in the battle at Heorot. The body gaped open
as it now suffered the stroke after death
from the hard-swung sword; he had severed the neck.

And above, the wise men who watched with Hrothgar
the depths of the pool descried soon enough
blood rising in the broken water
and marbling the surface. Seasoned warriors,
grey-headed, experienced, they spoke together,

said it seemed unlikely that they would see once more
the prince returning triumphant to seek out
their famous master. Many were persuaded
the she-wolf of the deep had done away with him.
The ninth hour had come; the keen-hearted Scyldings
abandoned the cliff-head; the kindly gold-giver
turned his face homeward. But the foreigners sat on,
staring at the pool with sickness at heart,
hoping they would look again on their beloved
   captain,
believing they would not.
                              The blood it had shed
made the sword dwindle into deadly icicles;
the war-tool wasted away. It was wonderful indeed
how it melted away entirely, as the ice does in the
   spring
when the Father unfastens the frost's grip,
unwinds the water's rope—He who watches over
the times and the seasons; He is the true God.

The Geat champion did not choose to take
any treasures from that hall, from the heaps he saw
   there,
other than that richly ornamented hilt,
and the head of Grendel. The engraved blade
had melted and burnt away: the blood was too hot,

the fiend that had died there too deadly by far.
The survivor of his enemies' onslaught in battle
now set to swimming, and struck up through the
   water;
both the deep reaches and the rough wave-swirl
were thoroughly cleansed, now the creature from the
   otherworld
drew breath no longer in this brief world's space.

Then the seamen's Helm came swimming up
strongly to land, delighting in his sea-trove,
those mighty burdens that he bore along with him.
They went to meet him, a manly company,
thanking God, glad of their lord,
seeing him safe and sound once more.
Quickly the champion's corselet and helmet
were loosened from him. The lake's waters,
sullied with blood, slept beneath the sky.

Then they turned away from there and retraced their
   steps,
pacing the familiar paths back again
as bold as kings, carefree at heart.
The carrying of the head from the cliff by the Mere
was no easy task for any of them,
brave as they were. They bore it up,

four of them, on a spear, and transported back
Grendel's head to the gold-giving hall.
Warrior-like they went, and it was not long
before they came, the fourteen bold Geats,
marching to the hall, and, among the company
walking across the land, their lord the tallest.
The earl of those thanes then entered boldly
—a man who had dared deeds and was adorned with
    their glory,
a man of prowess—to present himself to Hrothgar.
Then was the head of Grendel, held up by its locks,
manhandled in where men were drinking;
it was an ugly thing for the earls and their queen,
an awesome sight; they eyed it well.

Beowulf spoke, son of Edgetheow:
'Behold! What you see here, O son of Healfdene,
prince of the Scyldings, was pleasant freight for us:
—these trophies from the lake betoken victory!

　　　Not easily did I survive
the fight under water; I performed this deed
not without a struggle. Our strife had ended
at its very beginning if God had not saved me.
Nothing could I perform in that fight with Hrunting,
it had no effect, fine weapon though it be.

But the Guide of mankind granted me the sight
—He often brings aid to the friendless—
of a huge Giant-sword hanging on the wall,
ancient and shining—and I snatched up the weapon.
When the hour afforded, in that fight I slew
the keepers of the hall. The coiling-patterned
blade burnt all away, as the blood sprang forth,
the hottest ever shed; the hilt I took from them.
So I avenged the violent slaughter
and outrages against the Danes; indeed it was fitting.
Now, I say, you may sleep in Heorot
free from care—your company of warriors
and every man of your entire people,
both the young men and the guard. Gone is the need
to fear those fell attacks of former times
on the lives of your earls, my lord of the Scyldings.'

Then the golden hilt was given into the hand
of the older warrior, the white-haired leader.
A Giant had forged it. With the fall of the demons
it passed into the possession of the prince of the Danes,
this work of wonder-smiths. The world was rid
of that invidious enemy of God
and his mother also, with their murders upon them;
and the hilt now belonged to the best of the kings
who ruled the earth in all the North

and distributed treasure between the seas.
Hrothgar looked on that long-treasured hilt
before he spoke. The spring was cut on it
of the primal strife, with the destruction at last
of the race of Giants by the rushing Flood,
a terrible end. Estranged was that race
from the Lord of Eternity: the tide of water
was the final reward that the Ruler sent them.
On clear gold labels let into the cross-piece
it was rightly told in runic letters,
set down and sealed, for whose sake it was
that the sword was first forged, that finest of iron,
spiral-hilted, serpent-bladed.

                    At the speaking of the wise
son of Healfdene the hall was silent:
'He who has long tendered justice and truth to his
    people,
their shepherd from of old, surely may say this,
remembering all that's gone—that this man was born
to be the best of men. Beowulf, my friend,
your name shall resound in the nations of the earth
that are furthest away.

                  How wise you are to bear
your great strength to peaceably! I shall perform my
    vows
agreed in our forewords. It is granted to your people

that you shall live to be a long-standing comfort
and bulwark to the heroes.

                              Heremod was not so
for the honoured Scyldings, the sons of Edgewela:
his manhood brought not pleasure but a plague upon
   us,
death and destruction to the Danish tribes.
In his fits he would cut down his comrade in war
and his table-companion—until he turned away
from the feastings of men, that famous prince.
This though the Almighty had exalted him in the bliss
of strength and vigour, advancing him far
above all other men. Yet inwardly his heart-hoard
grew raw and blood-thirsty; no rings did he give
to the Danes for his honour. And he dwelt an outcast,
paid the penalty for his persecution of them
by a life of sorrow. Learn from this, Beowulf:
study openhandedness! It is for your ears that I relate
   this,
and I am old in winters.

                              It is wonderful to recount
how in his magnanimity the Almighty God
deals out wisdom, dominion and lordship
among mankind. The Master of all things
will sometimes allow to the soul of a man
of well-known kindred to wander in delight:

He will grant him earth's bliss in his own homeland,
the sway of the fortress-city of his people,
and will give him to rule regions of the world,
wide kingdoms: he cannot imagine,
in his unwisdom, that an end will come.
His life of bounty is not blighted by hint
of age or ailment; no evil care
darkens his mind, malice nowhere
bares the sword-edge, but sweetly the world
swings to his will; worse is not looked for.
At last his part of pride within him
waxes and climbs, the watchman of the soul
slumbering the while. That sleep is too deep,
tangled in its cares! Too close is the slayer
who shoots the wicked shaft from his bow!
For all his armour he is unable to protect himself:
the insidious bolt buries in his chest,
the crooked counsels of the accursed one.
What he has so long enjoyed he rejects as too little;
in niggardly anger renounces his lordly
gifts of gilt torques, forgets and misprises
his fore-ordained part, endowed thus by God,
the Master of Glory, with these great bounties.
And ultimately the end must come,
the frail house of flesh must crumble
and fall at its hour. Another then takes

the earl's inheritance; open-handedly
he gives out its treasure, regardless of fear.

Beloved Beowulf, best of warriors,
resist this deadly taint, take what is better,
your lasting profit. Put away arrogance,
noble fighter! The noon of your strength
shall last for a while now, but in a little time
sickness or a sword will strip it from you:
either enfolding flame or a flood's billow
or a knife-stab or the stoop of a spear
or the ugliness of age; or your eyes' brightness
lessens and grows dim. Death shall soon
have beaten you then, O brave warrior!

So it is with myself. I swayed the Ring-Danes
for fifty years here, defending them in war
with ash and with edge over the earth's breadth
against many nations; until I numbered at last
not a single adversary beneath the skies' expanse.
But what change of fortune befell me at my hearth
with the coming of Grendel; grief sprang from joy
when the old enemy entered our hall!
Great was the pain that persecution
thrust upon me. Thanks be to God,
the Lord everlasting, that I have lived until this day,

seen out this age of ancient strife
and set my gaze upon this gory head!
But join those who are seated, and rejoice in the feast,
O man clad in victory! We shall divide between us
many treasures when morning comes.'

The Geat went most gladly to take
his seat at the bench, at the bidding of the wise one.
Quite as before, the famous men,
guests of the hall, were handsomely feasted
on this new occasion. Then night's darkness
grew on the company. The guard arose,
for their wise leader wished to rest,
the grey-haired Scylding. The Geat was ready enough
to go to his bed too, brave shieldsman.

The bower-thane soon brought on his way
this fight-wearied and far-born man.
His courteous office was to care for all
a guest's necessities, such as at that day
the wants of a seafaring warrior might be.
The hero took his rest; the hall towered up
gilded, wide-gabled, its guest within sleeping
until the black raven blithe-hearted greeted
the heaven's gladness. Hastening, the sunlight

shook out above the shadows. Sharp were the bold
  ones,
each atheling eager to set off,
back to his homeland: the high-mettled stranger
wished to be forging far in his ship.
That hardy man ordered Hrunting to be carried
back to the son of Edgelaf, bade him accept again
his well-loved sword; said that he accounted it
formidable in the fight, a good friend in war,
thanked him for the loan of it, without the least
  finding fault
with the edge of that blade; ample was his spirit!

By then the fighting-men were fairly armed-up
and ready for the journey; the Joy of the Danes went,
a prince, to the high seat where Hrothgar was,
one hero brave in battle hailed the other.

Beowulf then spoke, son of Edgetheow.
'We now wish to say, seafarers who
are come from far, how keenly we desire
to return again to Hygelac. Here we were rightly,
royally, treated; you have entertained us well.
If I can ever on this earth earn of you,
O lord of men, more of your love
than I have so far done, by deeds of war,

I shall at once be ready. If ever I hear
that the neighbouring tribes intend your harm,
as those who hate you have done in the past,
I'll bring a thousand thanes and heroes
here to help you. As for Hygelac, I know
that the Lord of the Geats, Guide of his flock,
young though he is, will yield his support
both in words and deeds so I may do you honour
and bring you a grove of grey-tipped spears
and my strength in aid when you are short of men.
Further, when Hrethric shall have it in mind
to come, as a king's son, to the courts of the Geats
he shall find many friends there. Far countries are seen
to more advantage by a man of valour.'

Hrothgar spoke to him in answer:
'These words you have delivered, the Lord in His
    wisdom
put in your heart. I have heard no man
of the age that you are utter such wisdom.
You are rich in strength and ripe of mind,
you are wise in your utterance. If ever it should happen
that spear or other spike of battle,
sword or sickness, should sweep away
the son of Hrethel, your sovereign lord,
shepherd of his people, my opinion is clear,

that the Sea-Geats will not be seeking for a better
man to be their king and keep their war-hoard,
if you still have life and would like to rule
the kingdom of your kinsmen. As I come to know
your temper, dear Beowulf, the better it pleases me.
You have brought it about that both the peoples,
the Sea-Geats and the Spear-Danes,
shall share out peace; the shock of war,
the old sourness, shall cease between us.
So long as I shall rule the reaches of this kingdom
we shall exchange wealth; a chief shall greet
his fellow with gifts over the gannet's bath
as the ship with curved prow crosses the seas
with presents and pledges. Your people, I know,
always open-natured in the old manner,
are fast to friends and firm toward enemies.'

Then the Shield of the Heroes, Healfdene's son,
presented him with twelve new treasures in the hall,
bade him with these tokens betake himself
safe to his people; and soon return again.
Then that king of noble race, ruler of the Scyldings,
embraced and kissed that best of thanes,
taking him by the neck; tears fell from
the grey-haired one. With the wisdom of age
he foresaw two things, the second more likely,

that they would never again greet one another,
meet thus as heroes. The man was so dear to him
that he could not stop the surging in his breast;
but hidden in the heart, held fast in its strings,
a deep longing for this dearly loved man
burned against the blood.

PENGUIN 60s CLASSICS

PENGUIN 60s CLASSICS

READ MORE IN PENGUIN

For complete information about books available from Penguin and how to order them, please write to us at the appropriate address below. Please note that for copyright reasons the selection of books varies from country to country.

IN THE UNITED KINGDOM: Please write to *Dept. EP, Penguin Books Ltd, Bath Road, Harmondsworth, Middlesex UB7 0DA.*

IN THE UNITED STATES: Please write to *Consumer Sales, Penguin USA, P.O. Box 999, Dept. 17109, Bergenfield, New Jersey 07621-0120.* VISA and MasterCard holders call 1-800-253-6476 to order Penguin titles.

IN CANADA: Please write to *Penguin Books Canada Ltd, 10 Alcorn Avenue, Suite 300, Toronto, Ontario M4V 3B2.*

IN AUSTRALIA: Please write to *Penguin Books Australia Ltd, P.O. Box 257, Ringwood, Victoria 3134.*

IN NEW ZEALAND: Please write to *Penguin Books (NZ) Ltd, Private Bag 102902, North Shore Mail Centre, Auckland 10.*

IN INDIA: Please write to *Penguin Books India Pvt Ltd, 706 Eros Apartments, 56 Nehru Place, New Delhi 110 019.*

IN THE NETHERLANDS: Please write to *Penguin Books Netherlands bv, Postbus 3507, NL-1001 AH Amsterdam.*

IN GERMANY: Please write to *Penguin Books Deutschland GmbH, Metzlerstrasse 26, 60594 Frankfurt am Main.*

IN SPAIN: Please write to *Penguin Books S. A., Bravo Murillo 19, 1° B, 28015 Madrid.*

IN ITALY: Please write to *Penguin Italia s.r.l., Via Felice Casati 20, I-20124 Milano.*

IN FRANCE: Please write to *Penguin France S. A., 17 rue Lejeune, I-31000 Toulouse.*

IN JAPAN: Please write to *Penguin Books Japan, Ishikiribashi Building, 2-5-4, Suido, Bunkyo-ku, Tokyo 112.*

IN GREECE: Please write to *Penguin Hellas Ltd, Dimocritou 3, GR-106 71 Athens.*

IN SOUTH AFRICA: Please write to *Longman Penguin Southern Africa (Pty) Ltd, Private Bag X08, Bertsham 2013.*